Transportation & Communication Series

The Internet

Julie Douglas

Enslow Publishers, Inc.

40 Industrial Road	PO Box 38
Box 398	Aldershot
Berkeley Heights, NJ 07922	Hants GU12 6BP
USA	UK

http://www.enslow.com

Library of Congress Cataloging-in-Publication Data

Douglas, Julie.
   The Internet / Julie Douglas.
      p. cm. — (Transportation & communication series)
   Includes bibliographical references and index.
   Summary: Discusses the history, accessibility, and functioning of the Internet.
   ISBN 0-7660-1889-X
   1. Internet—Juvenile literature. [1. Internet.] I. Title. II. Series.
TK5105.875.I57 D67 2001
004.67'8—dc21   2001004010

Printed in the United States of America

10 9 8 7 6 5 4 3 2 1

To Our Readers: We have done our best to make sure all Internet addresses in this book were active and appropriate when we went to press. However, the author and the publisher have no control over and assume no liability for the material available on those Internet sites or on other Web sites they may link to. Any comments or suggestions can be sent by e-mail to comments@enslow.com or to the address on the back cover.

Illustration credits: Courtesy of Ask Jeeves Kids, p. 13; Courtesy of bugbios.com, p. 7 (bottom); Corel Corporation, pp. 4, 6 (top), 20, 24, 37; Courtesy of Cyberangels, p. 28; DiAMAR Interactive Corp, p. 35; Dover Publications, Inc., p. 16; Enslow Publishers, Inc., pp. 11 (bottom), 17, 19; Courtesy of Extension Entomology, Texas A&M University, p. 7 (top); Hemera Technologies, Inc. 1997-2000, pp. 1, 2, 5, 9, 10, (top), 11 (top), 12 (top), 15, 21, 22 (bottom), 23 (top), 25 (top), 27, 30, 31, 33, 36, 38; Courtesy of KidsClick!, p. 18; Kristin McCarthy, pp. 8, 25 (bottom), 26, 32; PhotoDisc, Inc., p. 34; Courtesy of Royal Ontario Museum Web site, p. 22 (top); Courtesy of the State of Alaska Online, p. 10 (bottom); Unisys Corporation, p. 14; Courtesy of the Web site of the North Dakota Governor's Office, p. 12 (bottom); Courtesy of www.fbi.gov, p. 23 (bottom); Courtesy of Yahooligans, p. 6 (bottom).

Cover Illustration: Kristin McCarthy

Contents

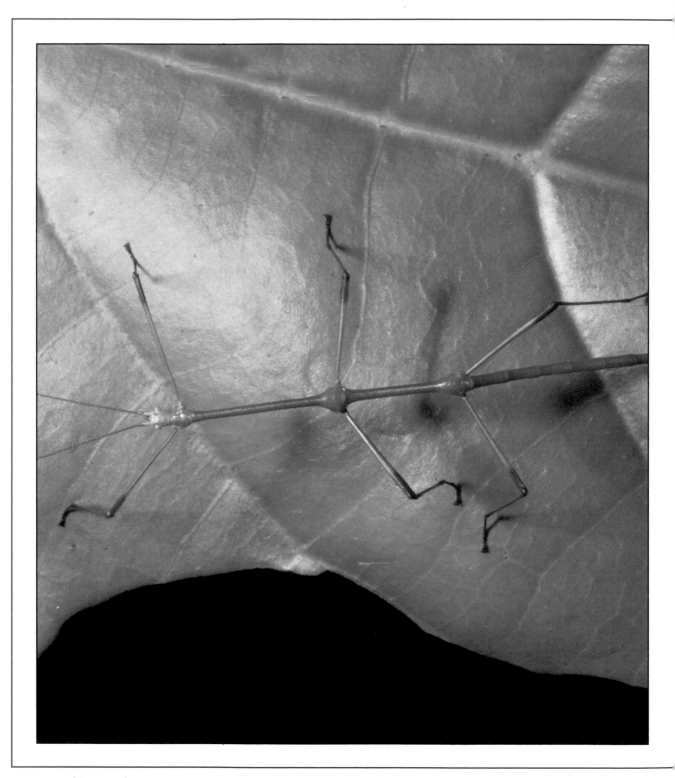

Chapter 1

A Class Uses the Internet

How did the Internet help a "stick" become a classroom pet? It began one morning at recess. A ball rolled to the edge of the playground. When the ball bumped the oak tree, a strange insect fell from a branch. It landed right on the playground. It was long and brown. At first the children thought it was a stick, but it moved a little as they watched it. They took the insect into the classroom. What was this thing that looked like a twig with tiny, black eyes and thin legs? Someone called it a "walking stick." What does it eat? Does it sting? Can we keep it? There were lots

Walking sticks look like twigs (left and above), and they can be green or brown.

5

Search engines are very useful. You can find many Web sites for the topic you are looking for by typing words into the search box.

of questions! But, the Internet had lots of answers.

The children began by logging on to the Internet. Next, they used a search engine to begin looking for Web sites about walking sticks. They typed "walking stick" into the search engine and found a list of Web sites about the insect. They clicked on a Web site. There they found photos of many kinds of walking sticks. Some walking sticks could grow to seven inches long! They learned that some people even keep walking sticks as pets. On another Web site the children read that walking sticks eat leaves. The insects stay hidden during the day and move around at night. The children bookmarked, or saved, some of the sites that were interesting so that they could go back and visit them later.

The children put the walking stick back in the oak tree near the playground. But their teacher said that a special kind of walking stick would make a good class pet. On the Internet, the children found the names of places that sold walking stick pets. They placed their order. Then they began to learn as much as they could about walking sticks. With the help of the Internet, a "stick" would be the new class pet.

Not only can you find pictures of walking sticks, but you can also find some facts about the insect.

Chapter 2

What is the Internet?

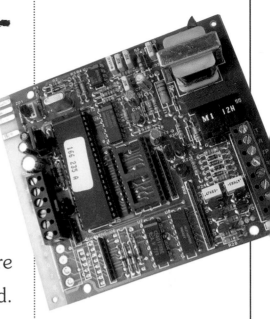

Think about the world around us. There are many places to go for the things we need. There are libraries, schools, stores, and hospitals. All of these places are connected to each other by streets. A computer network is like a network of streets. A network is a group of things that are joined together. A computer network is made of wire, phone lines, and even satellites. The Internet is made up of many computers connected to each other. The computers in homes, libraries, stores, and many other places are connected in this network. People can "travel" to places on the

Computer networks are made of many things such as a computer circuit board (above).

Internet using a computer. But they are not really going anywhere. The information is coming to them!

People can send each other letters and pictures using their computers. A person starts by using a computer to send a message to another computer. The message travels along a phone line until it reaches an Internet Service Provider (ISP). An ISP is a company that provides a connection to the Internet. The computer at the ISP quickly sends the message to a supercomputer. A supercomputer is a very big, fast computer. Supercomputers are in many places in the world. They are connected to many other ISPs. The message then travels from a supercomputer to another ISP and then to the other person's computer.

Computers can also communicate with

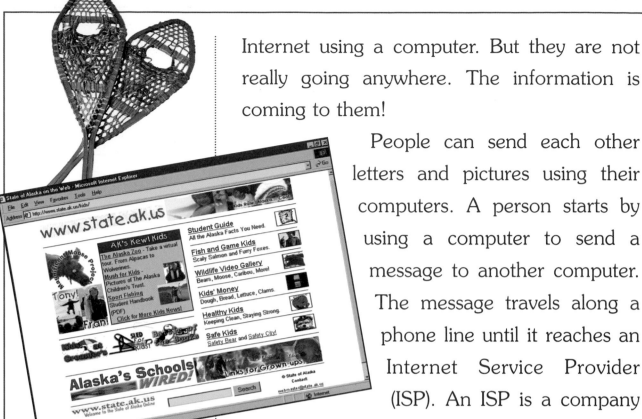

The Internet lets people travel all over the world without leaving their homes. A person could be sitting at home in Illinois and be able to go to Alaska!

each other. Many computers talk with other computers by using a modem. A modem is a device that sends information along telephone lines. Some computers "talk" by sending information through telephone lines. Others use cables and T1 lines. These lines carry even more information.

How does information travel through the phone lines? Words and pictures are broken into tiny electronic signals called packets. The packets are then sent by the computer through the phone lines. Along the way, machines called routers make sure the packets are going to the right place in the fastest way. When all of the packets make it to where they were sent, the computer puts them into the right order to make words and pictures.

People often talk about "the Web" when they use the Internet. The World Wide Web is

Computer networks can be made up of many computers. Here, five computers are connected in a network.

To go to a Web site, you can type the address into the address bar of the browser.

a part of the Internet. The World Wide Web (WWW) is a collection of pages, or documents. They are stored on computers all over the world. These pages can have pictures, graphics, movies, and music.

To go to a Web site, a person first types the Web address into the address bar of the browser. A browser is a computer program that lets a person get to Web sites on the World Wide Web. The browser sends a message to the server where the page is stored and asks for it. The server then sends the page back to the person's computer. The browser is able to read the information and show it on the computer screen. Web pages also have hypertext links that can be clicked. Hypertext links tell the computer how to go to a new site without having to type in the Web address. Links make it easy to get from one site to another.

Web sites have special addresses called uniform resource locators (URLs). The beginning part of the URL tells the computer how to get the document. Many URLs begin with *http://*. That stands for HyperText Transfer Protocol.

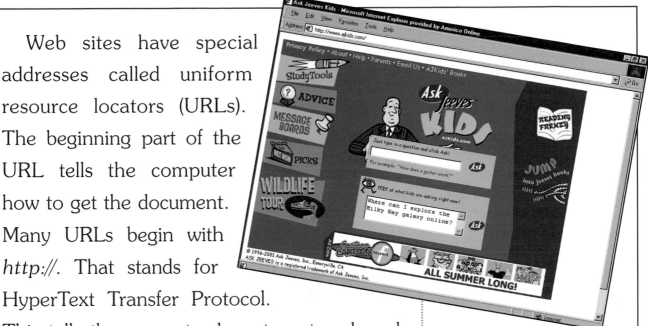

This tells the computer how to get and read the page. The first part of the Web address is called the host name. In most URLs this is *www*. The second part is called the domain name. It tells the name of the server where the page is stored. The third part is called the top-level domain name. For example, the *com* or *gov* of the URL.

The Internet can be used for learning new things, shopping, having fun, and talking with others. Although people still use books, telephones, and the mail, the Internet gives us another way to share information.

Web sites like Ask Jeeves are search engines. You can type in a word or group of words to find Web sites about your topic.

Chapter 3

The History of the Internet

People get information in many ways. There are books and magazines to read. People can listen to the radio and watch television. Or they can talk to each other. People mail letters to each other. Many people use e-mail to share news. They visit Web sites on the Internet to get facts. Computers are just another way to help people communicate.

The first computers were big machines. Only a few people knew how to use them. The computers were used by universities, large companies, and the government. People did not have computers in their homes.

Grace Hopper (left) stands next to one of the first computers. She helped to come up with the phrase "computer bug" after she found a moth in a computer. She also helped to develop a computer language called COBOL.

President Dwight D. Eisenhower.

In the late 1950s and early 1960s, the United States government wanted the big computers to be connected to each other. The government wanted a way for information to be shared and kept safe. President Dwight D. Eisenhower asked a group of scientists in the Department of Defense to work on new ways of using technology. Technology means using science or machines to solve problems. This group was called the Advanced Research Projects Agency (ARPA). The scientists connected computers from different parts of the United States to each other. They called the network ARPANET.

Dr. Robert E. Kahn and Dr. Vinton Cerf are computer scientists. They found a way to break information into packets that could be sent from one computer to another. Their system was called TCP/IP. That stands for Transmission Control Protocol/Internet Protocol. A protocol is a code, or set of rules, that computers use to "talk" to each other. All computers that are connected to the Internet must know these codes to send and get information. This system was so important that Dr. Cerf is sometimes called "the Father of the Internet."

In 1972, electronic mail, or e-mail, was invented by a computer engineer named Ray Tomlinson. People could send messages to each other over the Internet. More businesses and colleges began joining the networks. The National Science Foundation Network built five supercomputer centers. Computer

Here are the four computers that were connected to make up ARPANET.

The Original ARPANET

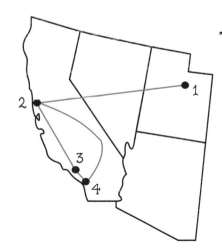

1. University of Utah
2. Stanford Research Center
3. University of California, Los Angeles
4. University of California, Santa Barbara

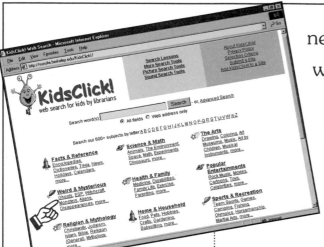

Links make it easy to go from one Web page to another without having to type in the URL in the address bar.

networks could now be connected with many other computer networks.

Computers at businesses and schools could be connected to each other. People began to call this network "the Internet" in the early 1980s. Soon other people wanted to connect to the Internet. New computers were smaller and easier to use. Many people had computers in their homes. They wanted a way to use the information on the Internet.

In 1990, a scientist named Timothy Berners-Lee had an idea that would help everyone use the Internet. He worked for the European Lab for Particle Physics, also called CERN. He developed a way to organize information on the Internet. It was called the World Wide Web. Pages of information could be stored on Web sites. These sites could also be linked to other sites. Going from one site to another was easy. A special computer language called HyperText Markup Language

(HTML) helped computers link information together. Instead of sending only words, computers could now send pictures, sounds, and videos.

Computer scientists were busy in the early 1990s. They were making computer programs that would help computers find and get pages stored on other computers. Search engines made looking for information as easy as typing in a word or phrase. In a little over 30 years, the Internet has become an exciting way to learn new things and share ideas with others. Now people all over the world use the Internet.

The National Science Foundation (NSF) built supercomputer centers so that many networks could be connected.

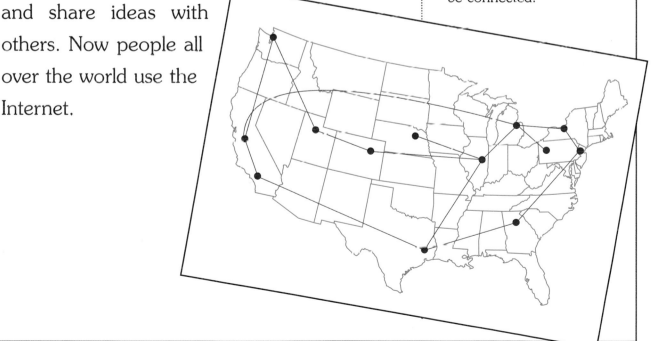

Chapter 4

People and the Internet

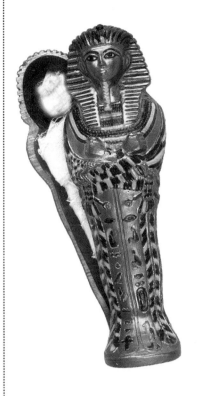

Not long ago, the Internet was used mostly by scientists. They wanted an easy way to share information. Now many people use the Internet to get and share information, too.

What Would You Do?

Let us say you need to do a report about mummies and you are allowed to use the Internet. What would you do? You could use a search engine to look for Web sites on the World Wide Web. Type the word "mummy" into the box on the search engine's screen. The search engine finds Web sites that will have information about mummies by checking

Many mummies were found in Egypt. Some were buried in pyramids like this one (left).

You can find out more about these waterfalls in Brazil (above) and other places on the Internet.

jokes, and puzzles. People at different computers, even far away from each other, can play games against one another online. Information about favorite sports and hobbies can be found on the Internet, too. Newspapers, magazines, and newsletters can be read online. Television shows have their own Web sites, too.

Many people have Web sites where they share information about themselves and things that interest them. Families and friends can post photos on their own Web sites. In chat rooms, people can talk with others who have an interest in a subject.

The Internet is not owned by anyone, but there are many people who work to keep it running. Engineers build computers and create software. Programmers "teach" computers how to do different jobs. Web designers create the Web pages that we visit. Web masters make sure the sites are working correctly. Technicians help people who are having problems with their computers or their Internet connection. Computer teachers show people how to use computers and the Internet. Computer scientists find new ways to use the Internet. As we find new ways to use the Internet, new jobs are made.

Some people have their own Web sites to share information about things that interest them.

My Scuba Trip!

Here is my Web site all about my very first scuba trip in a tropical paradise! We saw lots of great fish and coral. I can't wait to go on another trip next year. Next time we're going to visit my friend who lives in California and dive off the coast there. He said that you can scuba in the kelp beds and even swim with baby seals. It should be great! Until then, enjoy the photos from this trip.

Next =>

Chapter 5

Staying Safe Online

Staying safe when using the Internet is important. Think about the ways you stay safe. You do not talk to strangers. You do not take things from people that you do not know. You do not go into houses if you do not know the people living in them. When you feel uncomfortable because of something that is said or done, you tell an adult that you trust, like your parents or a teacher. Your family may have other special safety rules, too.

A trusted adult can help you stay safe. It is important not to keep secrets about what you are doing on the Internet. Tell an adult you trust if you see or hear anything that makes

You can stay safe on the Internet if you follow these rules.

Cyberangels has an "Internet Contract" that you and your family can sign.

you feel uncomfortable. Some families find it helpful to make an "Internet Contract" with each other. The family decides on rules that will help them use the Internet safely. All of the family members read the rules and sign the contract. An organization called Cyberangels has an agreement with good rules that you can print out. Following these rules will help you to stay safe online.

The Internet is full of new things to learn. There are many great Web sites to visit on the Internet. But, there are also sites on the Internet that are not good. Anyone can have a Web site where they can say anything—even things that are not true. It might be hard to figure out which Web sites have good information. Ask an adult to help you. The Internet also has sites for adults only. Ask an adult if you are not sure if a Web site is for adults or for kids.

The Internet can be a place to meet new people and talk about fun things. E-mail, chat rooms, and message boards are ways for people to talk with each other. To stay safe while talking to other people on the Internet, do not give your real name, address, or telephone number to anyone. Nicknames, called screen names, are used when talking with others online. This keeps your personal information safe. But using a nickname also

Keep these things in mind when you are on the Internet.

Be Smart and Stay Safe

- Do not keep secrets about what you are doing on the Internet.
- Tell an adult you trust if anything you see or hear makes you uncomfortable.
- Ask an adult if you are not sure if a Web site is for adults only or just for kids.
- Do not give your real name, address, or telephone number to anyone.
- Do not agree to meet anyone that you have met online.
- Do not send anyone your picture or invite them to your home.
- Tell an adult if someone offers to send you money or a gift.
- Ask an adult before ordering anything online.
- Be polite and use netiquette when talking to other people online.
- Being smart and staying safe can make "surfing the Net" even more fun.

The Internet can be lots of fun!

lets people pretend to be someone they are not. Most people on the Internet are probably who they say they are. Remember that people you meet online are really still strangers to you. Tell an adult if anything makes you uncomfortable. A trusted adult should always know who you are talking with online.

When you talk with someone online, it may seem like it would be fun to meet that person in real life. One of the most important rules of safety on the Internet is to never agree to meet anyone that you have met online. Never send anyone your picture, or invite someone to your home. Let an adult know if someone offers to send you money or a gift.

The Internet can be a fun place to shop. Ask an adult before ordering anything online. Most stores that sell goods online will need to get a credit card number from an adult, as well as other information. Only adults should give this information.

When people speak to each other, they

usually try to have good manners. They do not say hurtful or mean things. On the Internet, remember that you are speaking to another person, even though you cannot see that person. *Netiquette* means using your manners when you are online. Do not call names, and do not answer anyone who calls you a name. If a person uses bad language, threatens you, or says anything that makes you feel uncomfortable, let an adult know right away.

The Internet can be a fun place to explore. Being smart and staying safe can make "surfing the Net" even more fun.

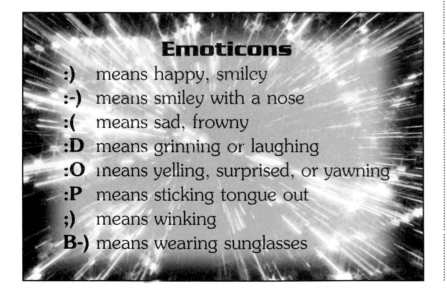

Emoticons
:)   means happy, smiley
:-) means smiley with a nose
:(means sad, frowny
:D   means grinning or laughing
:O   means yelling, surprised, or yawning
:P   means sticking tongue out
;)   means winking
B-) means wearing sunglasses

Emotion icons, or emoticons, are ways of saying how you feel when you talk to someone on the Internet. Instead of using words, you use symbols. Try making your own emoticons. (Turn the book sideways to view the faces.)

Chapter 6

The Internet of the Future

The Internet was not easy to use at first. Computers were big and cost a lot. Not many people knew how to use them. The idea of connecting computers together in a network was a very new idea in the early 1960s. When the scientists at ARPANET first developed the Internet, they probably could not imagine all the ways it would be used. But as scientists and engineers improved technology, the Internet became faster and easier to use.

New technology has changed the way people use the Internet. Fiber optics lets information travel faster between computers.

Surfing the Net has become faster with new technology.

33

This is the inside of a fiber optics cable.

Computers connected to the Internet, such as the one pictured right, are used all the time at home, school, and work.

Fiber optics are glass or plastic fibers in a cable that send light the length of the cable. New software lets people share words, pictures, videos, and sounds on the Internet. Software are programs that tell a computer what to do. E-mail is an easy way to talk with people anywhere in the world. Computers that are connected to the Internet are used at home, at school, in the library, and at work.

Someday in the future, your refrigerator might automatically e-mail the shopping list to the grocery store for you.

Someday in the future, astronauts (right) might be able to explore space through the use of the Internet.

The Internet is a helpful tool that people use in their everyday lives now. But how will the Internet be used in the future?

What if your washing machine knew when it was not working and could e-mail a message to a repairman by itself? Imagine a refrigerator that could e-mail your grocery list to the store. What if astronauts could explore far away planets using the Internet? Imagine visiting virtual 3-D (three-dimensional) places made of graphics and sound right on your computer.

What would it be like to wear clothing that carried a tiny computer and could be connected to the Internet? These are just some of the ideas people have for using the Internet in the future.

Engineers and scientists are working on machines that use the Internet to make our lives easier. Face-to-face e-mail would let you see the person you are talking to online.

Robots that are connected to the Internet are being tested. Cars that can drive themselves might be possible with the help of the Internet. Everything from wristwatches to spaceships may one day be connected to the Internet. We are only beginning to learn all of the ways that we can use computers and the Internet. New uses for the Internet are being invented everyday!

Someday cars might drive by themselves.

Web Site Guide

Here are some of the Web sites that are talked about in this book. To learn more, try searching using a search engine.

Cyberangels

<http://www.cyberangels.org/cdm/safety/agreement.html>

This site has a Family Internet Agreement that you and your family can use.

FBI-Kids Page

<http://www.fbi.gov/kids/k5th/kidsk5th.htm>

Take a field trip of the FBI by clicking on links.

Make Your Own Mummy

<http://www.rom.on.ca/egypt/mummy/mum1.html>

Mold a mummy out of clay.

Web Site Guide

BugBios

<http://www.insects.org/entophiles/phasmida/phas_001.html>

Learn about the walking stick insect.

Search Engines

Ask Jeeves for Kids

<http://www.ajkids.com>

KidsClick! Web search for kids by librarians

<http://sunsite.berkeley.edu/KidsClick!/>

Yahooligans

<http://www.yahooligans.com>

Timeline

1957—President Dwight D. Eisenhower sets up the Advanced Research Projects Agency (ARPA).

1960s—ARPANET, a network of computers at universities, begins.

1972—E-mail is invented by Ray Tomlinson.

1973—Dr. Robert Kahn and Dr. Vinton Cerf create Transmission Control Protocol/Internet Protocol (TCP/IP).

1980s—Many new networks are connected and are called "the Internet."

1990s—Internet becomes easier to use; People all over the world can be connected to the Internet.

1992—World Wide Web is developed by Tim Berners-Lee.

2001—New uses for the Internet are invented.

Words to Know

ARPANET—The network a group of scientists put together in the 1960s. This was the beginning of the Internet.

browser—A computer program that lets a person get to Web sites on the World Wide Web.

database—Where information is stored.

e-mail—Electronic mail, sending a message from one computer to another.

fiber optics—Glass or plastic fibers in a cable that send light the length of the cable.

graphics—Pictures made by a computer.

hypertext links—Links tell the computer how to go to a new Web site without having to type in the Web address.

HyperText Markup Language (HTML)—A special computer language that helps computers link information together.

Words to Know

Internet Service Provider (ISP)—A company that provides a connection to the Internet.

modem—A device that allows a computer to send data along a telephone line.

netiquette—Using manners while online.

network—Computers that are linked together.

online—Using a computer while it is connected to the Internet.

packets—Small pieces of information sent from one computer to another.

routers—Special computers that direct information as it travels between computers.

server—A server is a machine that provides services to other machines. The server machine finds the page you clicked on and sends it to your computer.

software—A program that tells a computer what to do.

Words to Know

supercomputer—A very big, fast computer.

technology—Using science or machines to solve problems.

Uniform Resource Locator (URL)—A Web site address.

World Wide Web (WWW)—Collection of information on computers that are connected to each other.

Learn More About
the Internet

Books

Brimner, Larry Dane. *The World Wide Web (A True Book)*. New York: Children's Press, 1997.

Gregory, Callie. *Jeeves, I'm Bored: 25 Internet Adventures for Kids*. Emeryville, Calif.: Ask Jeeves, Inc., 2000.

Jortberg, Charles. *The Internet*. Edina, Minn.: Abdo & Daughters, 1997.

Kalman, Bobbie. *The Computer From A to Z*. New York: Crabtree Publishing, 1999.

Leebow, Ken. *300 Incredible Things for Kids on the Internet*. Marietta, Ga.: VIP Publishing, 1999.

Steinhauser, Peggy. *Mousetracks: A Kid's Computer Idea Book*. Berkeley, Calif.: Tricycle Press, 1997.

Learn More About
the Internet

Internet Addresses

Brain Pop

<http://www.brainpop.com>

This site has short movies about the Internet and Online Safety.

How E-mail Works

<http://www.howstuffworks.com/email.htm>

Find out how e-mail works.

Internet

<http://www.howstuffworks.com/category.htm?cat=Intrnt>

This is a list of topics to choose from to learn more about the Internet.

Index

Index